Quantum Connections Manifestation Journal

A guided manifestation journal using the 33 x 3 method.

Leah Shoman

SACRED SCRIBE
publishing

Quantum Connections Manifestation Journal

Follow us @sacred.scribe.publishing
Tag us in your images #SacredScribePublishing
www.sacredscribepublishing.com

Published by Sacred Scribe Publishing LLC

Edited by Leah Shoman
Designs by Leah Shoman, Sacred Scribe Publishing LLC

ISBN 979-8-9879866-4-6

Printed and bound in China.

HOW TO USE

Quantum Connections Manifestation Journal

Unlock the power of the 33x3 Manifestation Method. Transform your desires into reality by writing them down 33 times for 3 days. This structured approach enhances focus and clarity, propelling you toward manifesting your intentions with precision.

Vision Board	First, you will use the vision board to help illustrate or write down what your manifestation looks like for you.
Offer Gratitude	Second, offer gratitude to show the Universe that you are grateful for what you currently have, in order to align your vibration with what you are calling in.
33 x 3 Manifesting	Thirdly, you will write out your manifestation 33 times for the next 3 days. While writing, hold the phrase in your mind, *"I am so happy and grateful now that I have..."*
Soul Reflection	Lastly, reflect on this manifestation process and ready yourself for your next journey.

DATE

/ /

Offer Gratitude

3 THINGS I AM FEELING TODAY

POSITIVE AFFIRMATION

3 THINGS I AM CURRENTLY GRATEFUL FOR

1 ______

2 ______

3 ______

SOMETHING I AM ALREADY PROUD OF

______

HOW I FEEL NOW	HOW I WANT TO FEEL

MY INTENTION FOR THIS MANIFESTATION

______

______

WHY IS THIS MANIFESTATION IMPORTANT TO ME?

Manifest

DATE

/ /

I am so happy and grateful now that I have...

1

2

3

4

5

6

7

8

9

10

11

12

13

14

15

16

17

18

19

20

21

22

23

24

25

26

27

28

29

30

31

32

33

Manifest

DATE

/ /

I am so happy and grateful now that I have...

1
2
3
4
5
6
7
8
9
10
11
12
13
14
15
16
17
18
19
20
21
22
23
24
25
26
27
28
29
30
31
32
33

Manifest

DATE

/ /

I am so happy and grateful now that I have...

1

2

3

4

5

6

7

8

9

10

11

12

13

14

15

16

17

18

19

20

21

22

23

24

25

26

27

28

29

30

31

32

33

DATE

/ /

Soul Reflection

3 CHANGES I OBSERVED AFTER MANIFESTING

1 ______

2 ______

3 ______

3 THINGS I LEARNED IN THIS PROCESS?

1 ______

2 ______

3 ______

3 CHALLENGES I FACED?

1 ______

2 ______

3 ______

AFTER MANIFESTING...

I SEE	I FEEL	I HAVE

MANIFESTATION HIGHLIGHTS

Notes

DATE

/ /

extra thoughts

Notes

DATE

/ /

extra thoughts

DATE

/ /

My Vision Board

what I envision my life will look like after this manifestation

career & finances

love & travel

home & family

spiritual & wellness

friends & connections

DATE

/ /

Offer Gratitude

3 THINGS I AM FEELING TODAY

POSITIVE AFFIRMATION

3 THINGS I AM CURRENTLY GRATEFUL FOR

1

2

3

SOMETHING I AM ALREADY PROUD OF

HOW I FEEL NOW

HOW I WANT TO FEEL

MY INTENTION FOR THIS MANIFESTATION

WHY IS THIS MANIFESTATION IMPORTANT TO ME?

Manifest

DATE

/ /

I am so happy and grateful now that I have...

1
2
3
4
5
6
7
8
9
10
11
12
13
14
15
16
17
18
19
20
21
22
23
24
25
26
27
28
29
30
31
32
33

Manifest

DATE

/ /

I am so happy and grateful now that I have...

1
2
3
4
5
6
7
8
9
10
11
12
13
14
15
16
17
18
19
20
21
22
23
24
25
26
27
28
29
30
31
32
33

Manifest

DATE

/ /

I am so happy and grateful now that I have...

1
2
3
4
5
6
7
8
9
10
11
12
13
14
15
16
17
18
19
20
21
22
23
24
25
26
27
28
29
30
31
32
33

DATE

/ /

Soul Reflection

3 CHANGES I OBSERVED AFTER MANIFESTING

1 ________________

2 ________________

3 ________________

3 THINGS I LEARNED IN THIS PROCESS?

1 ________________

2 ________________

3 ________________

3 CHALLENGES I FACED?

1 ________________

2 ________________

3 ________________

AFTER MANIFESTING...

I SEE	I FEEL	I HAVE

MANIFESTATION HIGHLIGHTS

Notes

DATE

/ /

extra thoughts

Notes

DATE

/ /

extra thoughts

DATE

/ /

My Vision Board

what I envision my life will look like after this manifestation

career & finances

love & travel

home & family

spiritual & wellness

friends & connections

DATE

/ /

Offer Gratitude

3 THINGS I AM FEELING TODAY

POSITIVE AFFIRMATION

3 THINGS I AM CURRENTLY GRATEFUL FOR

1 ____________________

2 ____________________

3 ____________________

SOMETHING I AM ALREADY PROUD OF

HOW I FEEL NOW

HOW I WANT TO FEEL

MY INTENTION FOR THIS MANIFESTATION

WHY IS THIS MANIFESTATION IMPORTANT TO ME?

Manifest

DATE

/ /

I am so happy and grateful now that I have...

1

2

3

4

5

6

7

8

9

10

11

12

13

14

15

16

17

18

19

20

21

22

23

24

25

26

27

28

29

30

31

32

33

Manifest

DATE

/ /

I am so happy and grateful now that I have...

1
2
3
4
5
6
7
8
9
10
11
12
13
14
15
16
17
18
19
20
21
22
23
24
25
26
27
28
29
30
31
32
33

Manifest

DATE

/ /

I am so happy and grateful now that I have...

1

2

3

4

5

6

7

8

9

10

11

12

13

14

15

16

17

18

19

20

21

22

23

24

25

26

27

28

29

30

31

32

33

DATE

/ /

Soul Reflection

3 CHANGES I OBSERVED AFTER MANIFESTING

1 ____________________

2 ____________________

3 ____________________

3 THINGS I LEARNED IN THIS PROCESS?

1 ____________________

2 ____________________

3 ____________________

3 CHALLENGES I FACED?

1 ____________________

2 ____________________

3 ____________________

AFTER MANIFESTING...

I SEE	I FEEL	I HAVE

MANIFESTATION HIGHLIGHTS

Notes

DATE

/ /

extra thoughts

Notes

DATE

/ /

extra thoughts

DATE

/ /

My Vision Board

what I envision my life will look like after this manifestation

career & finances

love & travel

home & family

spiritual & wellness

friends & connections

DATE

/ /

Offer Gratitude

3 THINGS I AM FEELING TODAY

POSITIVE AFFIRMATION

3 THINGS I AM CURRENTLY GRATEFUL FOR

1

2

3

SOMETHING I AM ALREADY PROUD OF

HOW I FEEL NOW

HOW I WANT TO FEEL

MY INTENTION FOR THIS MANIFESTATION

WHY IS THIS MANIFESTATION IMPORTANT TO ME?

Manifest

DATE

/ /

I am so happy and grateful now that I have...

1

2

3

4

5

6

7

8

9

10

11

12

13

14

15

16

17

18

19

20

21

22

23

24

25

26

27

28

29

30

31

32

33

Manifest

DATE

/ /

I am so happy and grateful now that I have...

1 ______

2 ______

3 ______

4 ______

5 ______

6 ______

7 ______

8 ______

9 ______

10 ______

11 ______

12 ______

13 ______

14 ______

15 ______

16 ______

17 ______

18 ______

19 ______

20 ______

21 ______

22 ______

23 ______

24 ______

25 ______

26 ______

27 ______

28 ______

29 ______

30 ______

31 ______

32 ______

33 ______

Manifest

DATE
/ /

I am so happy and grateful now that I have...

1
2
3
4
5
6
7
8
9
10
11
12
13
14
15
16
17
18
19
20
21
22
23
24
25
26
27
28
29
30
31
32
33

DATE

/ /

Soul Reflection

3 CHANGES I OBSERVED AFTER MANIFESTING

1 ______

2 ______

3 ______

3 THINGS I LEARNED IN THIS PROCESS?

1 ______

2 ______

3 ______

3 CHALLENGES I FACED?

1 ______

2 ______

3 ______

AFTER MANIFESTING...

I SEE	I FEEL	I HAVE

MANIFESTATION HIGHLIGHTS

Notes

DATE

/ /

extra thoughts

Notes

DATE

/ /

extra thoughts

DATE

/ /

My Vision Board

what I envision my life will look like after this manifestation

career & finances

love & travel

home & family

spiritual & wellness

friends & connections

DATE

/ /

Offer Gratitude

3 THINGS I AM FEELING TODAY

POSITIVE AFFIRMATION

3 THINGS I AM CURRENTLY GRATEFUL FOR

1 __________

2 __________

3 __________

SOMETHING I AM ALREADY PROUD OF

HOW I FEEL NOW

HOW I WANT TO FEEL

MY INTENTION FOR THIS MANIFESTATION

WHY IS THIS MANIFESTATION IMPORTANT TO ME?

Manifest

DATE

/ /

I am so happy and grateful now that I have...

1
2
3
4
5
6
7
8
9
10
11
12
13
14
15
16
17
18
19
20
21
22
23
24
25
26
27
28
29
30
31
32
33

Manifest

DATE

/ /

I am so happy and grateful now that I have...

1
2
3
4
5
6
7
8
9
10
11
12
13
14
15
16
17
18
19
20
21
22
23
24
25
26
27
28
29
30
31
32
33

Manifest

DATE
/ /

I am so happy and grateful now that I have...

1
2
3
4
5
6
7
8
9
10
11
12
13
14
15
16
17
18
19
20
21
22
23
24
25
26
27
28
29
30
31
32
33

DATE

/ /

Soul Reflection

3 CHANGES I OBSERVED AFTER MANIFESTING

1 ____

2 ____

3 ____

3 THINGS I LEARNED IN THIS PROCESS?

1 ____

2 ____

3 ____

3 CHALLENGES I FACED?

1 ____

2 ____

3 ____

AFTER MANIFESTING...

I SEE	I FEEL	I HAVE

MANIFESTATION HIGHLIGHTS

Notes

DATE

/ /

extra thoughts

Notes

DATE

/ /

extra thoughts

DATE

/ /

My Vision Board

what I envision my life will look like after this manifestation

career & finances

love & travel

home & family

spiritual & wellness

friends & connections

DATE

/ /

Offer Gratitude

3 THINGS I AM FEELING TODAY

POSITIVE AFFIRMATION

3 THINGS I AM CURRENTLY GRATEFUL FOR

1 __________

2 __________

3 __________

SOMETHING I AM ALREADY PROUD OF

HOW I FEEL NOW

HOW I WANT TO FEEL

MY INTENTION FOR THIS MANIFESTATION

WHY IS THIS MANIFESTATION IMPORTANT TO ME?

Manifest

DATE

/ /

I am so happy and grateful now that I have...

1 ___

2 ___

3 ___

4 ___

5 ___

6 ___

7 ___

8 ___

9 ___

10 ___

11 ___

12 ___

13 ___

14 ___

15 ___

16 ___

17 ___

18 ___

19 ___

20 ___

21 ___

22 ___

23 ___

24 ___

25 ___

26 ___

27 ___

28 ___

29 ___

30 ___

31 ___

32 ___

33 ___

Manifest

DATE
/ /

I am so happy and grateful now that I have...

1
2
3
4
5
6
7
8
9
10
11
12
13
14
15
16
17
18
19
20
21
22
23
24
25
26
27
28
29
30
31
32
33

Manifest

DATE

/ /

I am so happy and grateful now that I have...

1
2
3
4
5
6
7
8
9
10
11
12
13
14
15
16
17
18
19
20
21
22
23
24
25
26
27
28
29
30
31
32
33

DATE

/ /

Soul Reflection

3 CHANGES I OBSERVED AFTER MANIFESTING

1 ____________________

2 ____________________

3 ____________________

3 THINGS I LEARNED IN THIS PROCESS?

1 ____________________

2 ____________________

3 ____________________

3 CHALLENGES I FACED?

1 ____________________

2 ____________________

3 ____________________

AFTER MANIFESTING...

I SEE	I FEEL	I HAVE

MANIFESTATION HIGHLIGHTS

Notes

DATE

/ /

extra thoughts

Notes

DATE

/ /

extra thoughts

DATE

/ /

My Vision Board

what I envision my life will look like after this manifestation

career & finances

love & travel

home & family

spiritual & wellness

friends & connections

DATE

/ /

Offer Gratitude

3 THINGS I AM FEELING TODAY

POSITIVE AFFIRMATION

3 THINGS I AM CURRENTLY GRATEFUL FOR

1 ____________________

2 ____________________

3 ____________________

SOMETHING I AM ALREADY PROUD OF

____

HOW I FEEL NOW	HOW I WANT TO FEEL

MY INTENTION FOR THIS MANIFESTATION

____

____

WHY IS THIS MANIFESTATION IMPORTANT TO ME?

Manifest

DATE

/ /

I am so happy and grateful now that I have...

1

2

3

4

5

6

7

8

9

10

11

12

13

14

15

16

17

18

19

20

21

22

23

24

25

26

27

28

29

30

31

32

33

Manifest

DATE

/ /

I am so happy and grateful now that I have...

1
2
3
4
5
6
7
8
9
10
11
12
13
14
15
16
17
18
19
20
21
22
23
24
25
26
27
28
29
30
31
32
33

Manifest

DATE

/ /

I am so happy and grateful now that I have...

1
2
3
4
5
6
7
8
9
10
11
12
13
14
15
16
17
18
19
20
21
22
23
24
25
26
27
28
29
30
31
32
33

DATE

/ /

Soul Reflection

3 CHANGES I OBSERVED AFTER MANIFESTING

1 _____

2 _____

3 _____

3 THINGS I LEARNED IN THIS PROCESS?

1 _____

2 _____

3 _____

3 CHALLENGES I FACED?

1 _____

2 _____

3 _____

AFTER MANIFESTING...

I SEE	I FEEL	I HAVE

MANIFESTATION HIGHLIGHTS

Notes

DATE

/ /

extra thoughts

Notes

DATE
/ /

extra thoughts

DATE

/ /

My Vision Board

what I envision my life will look like after this manifestation

career & finances

love & travel

home & family

spiritual & wellness

friends & connections

DATE

/ /

Offer Gratitude

3 THINGS I AM FEELING TODAY

POSITIVE AFFIRMATION

3 THINGS I AM CURRENTLY GRATEFUL FOR

1

2

3

SOMETHING I AM ALREADY PROUD OF

HOW I FEEL NOW	HOW I WANT TO FEEL

MY INTENTION FOR THIS MANIFESTATION

WHY IS THIS MANIFESTATION IMPORTANT TO ME?

Manifest

DATE

/ /

I am so happy and grateful now that I have...

Manifest

DATE

/ /

I am so happy and grateful now that I have...

1
2
3
4
5
6
7
8
9
10
11
12
13
14
15
16
17
18
19
20
21
22
23
24
25
26
27
28
29
30
31
32
33

Manifest

DATE

/ /

I am so happy and grateful now that I have...

1
2
3
4
5
6
7
8
9
10
11
12
13
14
15
16
17
18
19
20
21
22
23
24
25
26
27
28
29
30
31
32
33

DATE

/ /

Soul Reflection

3 CHANGES I OBSERVED AFTER MANIFESTING

1 ______________________________

2 ______________________________

3 ______________________________

3 THINGS I LEARNED IN THIS PROCESS?

1 ______________________________

2 ______________________________

3 ______________________________

3 CHALLENGES I FACED?

1 ______________________________

2 ______________________________

3 ______________________________

AFTER MANIFESTING...

I SEE	I FEEL	I HAVE

MANIFESTATION HIGHLIGHTS

Notes

DATE

/ /

extra thoughts

Notes

DATE

/ /

extra thoughts

DATE

/ /

My Vision Board

what I envision my life will look like after this manifestation

career & finances

love & travel

home & family

spiritual & wellness

friends & connections

DATE

/ /

Offer Gratitude

3 THINGS I AM FEELING TODAY

POSITIVE AFFIRMATION

3 THINGS I AM CURRENTLY GRATEFUL FOR

1

2

3

SOMETHING I AM ALREADY PROUD OF

HOW I FEEL NOW

HOW I WANT TO FEEL

MY INTENTION FOR THIS MANIFESTATION

WHY IS THIS MANIFESTATION IMPORTANT TO ME?

Manifest

DATE
/ /

I am so happy and grateful now that I have...

1
2
3
4
5
6
7
8
9
10
11
12
13
14
15
16
17
18
19
20
21
22
23
24
25
26
27
28
29
30
31
32
33

Manifest

DATE

/ /

I am so happy and grateful now that I have...

1

2

3

4

5

6

7

8

9

10

11

12

13

14

15

16

17

18

19

20

21

22

23

24

25

26

27

28

29

30

31

32

33

Manifest

DATE

/ /

I am so happy and grateful now that I have...

1
2
3
4
5
6
7
8
9
10
11
12
13
14
15
16
17
18
19
20
21
22
23
24
25
26
27
28
29
30
31
32
33

DATE

/ /

Soul Reflection

3 CHANGES I OBSERVED AFTER MANIFESTING

1 ____________________

2 ____________________

3 ____________________

3 THINGS I LEARNED IN THIS PROCESS?

1 ____________________

2 ____________________

3 ____________________

3 CHALLENGES I FACED?

1 ____________________

2 ____________________

3 ____________________

AFTER MANIFESTING...

I SEE	I FEEL	I HAVE

MANIFESTATION HIGHLIGHTS

Notes

DATE

/ /

extra thoughts

Notes

DATE
/ /

extra thoughts

DATE

/ /

My Vision Board

what I envision my life will look like after this manifestation

career & finances

love & travel

home & family

spiritual & wellness

friends & connections

DATE

/ /

Offer Gratitude

3 THINGS I AM FEELING TODAY

POSITIVE AFFIRMATION

3 THINGS I AM CURRENTLY GRATEFUL FOR

1 __________

2 __________

3 __________

SOMETHING I AM ALREADY PROUD OF

HOW I FEEL NOW

HOW I WANT TO FEEL

MY INTENTION FOR THIS MANIFESTATION

WHY IS THIS MANIFESTATION IMPORTANT TO ME?

Manifest

DATE

/ /

I am so happy and grateful now that I have...

1
2
3
4
5
6
7
8
9
10
11
12
13
14
15
16
17
18
19
20
21
22
23
24
25
26
27
28
29
30
31
32
33

Manifest

DATE

/ /

I am so happy and grateful now that I have...

1

2

3

4

5

6

7

8

9

10

11

12

13

14

15

16

17

18

19

20

21

22

23

24

25

26

27

28

29

30

31

32

33

Manifest

DATE

/ /

I am so happy and grateful now that I have...

1
2
3
4
5
6
7
8
9
10
11
12
13
14
15
16
17
18
19
20
21
22
23
24
25
26
27
28
29
30
31
32
33

DATE

/ /

Soul Reflection

3 CHANGES I OBSERVED AFTER MANIFESTING

1 ____________________

2 ____________________

3 ____________________

3 THINGS I LEARNED IN THIS PROCESS?

1 ____________________

2 ____________________

3 ____________________

3 CHALLENGES I FACED?

1 ____________________

2 ____________________

3 ____________________

AFTER MANIFESTING...

I SEE	I FEEL	I HAVE

MANIFESTATION HIGHLIGHTS

Notes

DATE

/ /

extra thoughts

Notes

DATE

/ /

extra thoughts

DATE

/ /

My Vision Board

what I envision my life will look like after this manifestation

career & finances

love & travel

home & family

spiritual & wellness

friends & connections

DATE

/ /

Offer Gratitude

3 THINGS I AM FEELING TODAY

POSITIVE AFFIRMATION

3 THINGS I AM CURRENTLY GRATEFUL FOR

1

2

3

SOMETHING I AM ALREADY PROUD OF

HOW I FEEL NOW

HOW I WANT TO FEEL

MY INTENTION FOR THIS MANIFESTATION

WHY IS THIS MANIFESTATION IMPORTANT TO ME?

Manifest

DATE

/ /

I am so happy and grateful now that I have...

1
2
3
4
5
6
7
8
9
10
11
12
13
14
15
16
17
18
19
20
21
22
23
24
25
26
27
28
29
30
31
32
33

Manifest

DATE

/ /

I am so happy and grateful now that I have...

1

2

3

4

5

6

7

8

9

10

11

12

13

14

15

16

17

18

19

20

21

22

23

24

25

26

27

28

29

30

31

32

33

Manifest

DATE

/ /

I am so happy and grateful now that I have...

1
2
3
4
5
6
7
8
9
10
11
12
13
14
15
16
17
18
19
20
21
22
23
24
25
26
27
28
29
30
31
32
33

DATE

/ /

Soul Reflection

3 CHANGES I OBSERVED AFTER MANIFESTING

1 __________

2 __________

3 __________

3 THINGS I LEARNED IN THIS PROCESS?

1 __________

2 __________

3 __________

3 CHALLENGES I FACED?

1 __________

2 __________

3 __________

AFTER MANIFESTING...

I SEE	I FEEL	I HAVE

MANIFESTATION HIGHLIGHTS

Notes

DATE

/ /

extra thoughts

Notes

DATE

/ /

extra thoughts

DATE

/ /

My Vision Board

what I envision my life will look like after this manifestation

career & finances

love & travel

home & family

spiritual & wellness

friends & connections

DATE

/ /

Offer Gratitude

3 THINGS I AM FEELING TODAY

POSITIVE AFFIRMATION

3 THINGS I AM CURRENTLY GRATEFUL FOR

1 __________

2 __________

3 __________

SOMETHING I AM ALREADY PROUD OF

HOW I FEEL NOW	HOW I WANT TO FEEL

MY INTENTION FOR THIS MANIFESTATION

WHY IS THIS MANIFESTATION IMPORTANT TO ME?

Manifest

DATE

/ /

I am so happy and grateful now that I have...

1
2
3
4
5
6
7
8
9
10
11
12
13
14
15
16
17
18
19
20
21
22
23
24
25
26
27
28
29
30
31
32
33

Manifest

DATE

/ /

I am so happy and grateful now that I have...

1
2
3
4
5
6
7
8
9
10
11
12
13
14
15
16
17
18
19
20
21
22
23
24
25
26
27
28
29
30
31
32
33

Manifest

DATE

/ /

I am so happy and grateful now that I have...

1

2

3

4

5

6

7

8

9

10

11

12

13

14

15

16

17

18

19

20

21

22

23

24

25

26

27

28

29

30

31

32

33

DATE

/ /

Soul Reflection

3 CHANGES I OBSERVED AFTER MANIFESTING

1 ____________________

2 ____________________

3 ____________________

3 THINGS I LEARNED IN THIS PROCESS?

1 ____________________

2 ____________________

3 ____________________

3 CHALLENGES I FACED?

1 ____________________

2 ____________________

3 ____________________

AFTER MANIFESTING...

I SEE	I FEEL	I HAVE

MANIFESTATION HIGHLIGHTS

Notes

DATE

/ /

extra thoughts

Notes

DATE

/ /

extra thoughts

DATE

/ /

My Vision Board

what I envision my life will look like after this manifestation

career & finances

love & travel

home & family

spiritual & wellness

friends & connections

DATE

/ /

Offer Gratitude

3 THINGS I AM FEELING TODAY

POSITIVE AFFIRMATION

3 THINGS I AM CURRENTLY GRATEFUL FOR

1

2

3

SOMETHING I AM ALREADY PROUD OF

HOW I FEEL NOW

HOW I WANT TO FEEL

MY INTENTION FOR THIS MANIFESTATION

WHY IS THIS MANIFESTATION IMPORTANT TO ME?

Manifest

DATE

/ /

I am so happy and grateful now that I have...

1
2
3
4
5
6
7
8
9
10
11
12
13
14
15
16
17
18
19
20
21
22
23
24
25
26
27
28
29
30
31
32
33

Manifest

DATE

/ /

I am so happy and grateful now that I have...

1 __________

2 __________

3 __________

4 __________

5 __________

6 __________

7 __________

8 __________

9 __________

10 __________

11 __________

12 __________

13 __________

14 __________

15 __________

16 __________

17 __________

18 __________

19 __________

20 __________

21 __________

22 __________

23 __________

24 __________

25 __________

26 __________

27 __________

28 __________

29 __________

30 __________

31 __________

32 __________

33 __________

Manifest

DATE
/ /

I am so happy and grateful now that I have...

1
2
3
4
5
6
7
8
9
10
11
12
13
14
15
16
17
18
19
20
21
22
23
24
25
26
27
28
29
30
31
32
33

DATE

/ /

Soul Reflection

3 CHANGES I OBSERVED AFTER MANIFESTING

1 ______

2 ______

3 ______

3 THINGS I LEARNED IN THIS PROCESS?

1 ______

2 ______

3 ______

3 CHALLENGES I FACED?

1 ______

2 ______

3 ______

AFTER MANIFESTING...

I SEE	I FEEL	I HAVE

MANIFESTATION HIGHLIGHTS

Notes

DATE

/ /

extra thoughts

Notes

DATE

/ /

extra thoughts

DATE

/ /

My Vision Board

what I envision my life will look like after this manifestation

career & finances

love & travel

home & family

spiritual & wellness

friends & connections

DATE

/ /

Offer Gratitude

3 THINGS I AM FEELING TODAY

POSITIVE AFFIRMATION

3 THINGS I AM CURRENTLY GRATEFUL FOR

1 ______

2 ______

3 ______

SOMETHING I AM ALREADY PROUD OF

______

HOW I FEEL NOW

HOW I WANT TO FEEL

MY INTENTION FOR THIS MANIFESTATION

______

______

WHY IS THIS MANIFESTATION IMPORTANT TO ME?

Manifest

DATE

/ /

I am so happy and grateful now that I have...

1

2

3

4

5

6

7

8

9

10

11

12

13

14

15

16

17

18

19

20

21

22

23

24

25

26

27

28

29

30

31

32

33

Manifest

DATE

/ /

I am so happy and grateful now that I have...

1
2
3
4
5
6
7
8
9
10
11
12
13
14
15
16
17
18
19
20
21
22
23
24
25
26
27
28
29
30
31
32
33

Manifest

DATE

/ /

I am so happy and grateful now that I have...

1
2
3
4
5
6
7
8
9
10
11
12
13
14
15
16
17
18
19
20
21
22
23
24
25
26
27
28
29
30
31
32
33

DATE

/ /

Soul Reflection

3 CHANGES I OBSERVED AFTER MANIFESTING

1 ______

2 ______

3 ______

3 THINGS I LEARNED IN THIS PROCESS?

1 ______

2 ______

3 ______

3 CHALLENGES I FACED?

1 ______

2 ______

3 ______

AFTER MANIFESTING...

I SEE	I FEEL	I HAVE

MANIFESTATION HIGHLIGHTS

Notes

DATE

/ /

extra thoughts

Notes

DATE

/ /

extra thoughts

DATE

/ /

My Vision Board

what I envision my life will look like after this manifestation

career & finances

love & travel

home & family

spiritual & wellness

friends & connections

DATE

/ /

Offer Gratitude

3 THINGS I AM FEELING TODAY

POSITIVE AFFIRMATION

3 THINGS I AM CURRENTLY GRATEFUL FOR

1

2

3

SOMETHING I AM ALREADY PROUD OF

HOW I FEEL NOW

HOW I WANT TO FEEL

MY INTENTION FOR THIS MANIFESTATION

WHY IS THIS MANIFESTATION IMPORTANT TO ME?

Manifest

DATE

/ /

I am so happy and grateful now that I have...

1

2

3

4

5

6

7

8

9

10

11

12

13

14

15

16

17

18

19

20

21

22

23

24

25

26

27

28

29

30

31

32

33

Manifest

DATE

/ /

I am so happy and grateful now that I have...

1
2
3
4
5
6
7
8
9
10
11
12
13
14
15
16
17
18
19
20
21
22
23
24
25
26
27
28
29
30
31
32
33

Manifest

DATE

/ /

I am so happy and grateful now that I have...

1
2
3
4
5
6
7
8
9
10
11
12
13
14
15
16
17
18
19
20
21
22
23
24
25
26
27
28
29
30
31
32
33

DATE

/ /

Soul Reflection

3 CHANGES I OBSERVED AFTER MANIFESTING

1 ____________________

2 ____________________

3 ____________________

3 THINGS I LEARNED IN THIS PROCESS?

1 ____________________

2 ____________________

3 ____________________

3 CHALLENGES I FACED?

1 ____________________

2 ____________________

3 ____________________

AFTER MANIFESTING...

I SEE	I FEEL	I HAVE

MANIFESTATION HIGHLIGHTS

Notes

DATE

/ /

extra thoughts

Notes

DATE

/ /

extra thoughts

DATE

/ /

My Vision Board

what I envision my life will look like after this manifestation

career & finances

love & travel

home & family

spiritual & wellness

friends & connections

DATE

/ /

Offer Gratitude

3 THINGS I AM FEELING TODAY

POSITIVE AFFIRMATION

3 THINGS I AM CURRENTLY GRATEFUL FOR

1

2

3

SOMETHING I AM ALREADY PROUD OF

HOW I FEEL NOW	HOW I WANT TO FEEL

MY INTENTION FOR THIS MANIFESTATION

WHY IS THIS MANIFESTATION IMPORTANT TO ME?

Manifest

DATE

/ /

I am so happy and grateful now that I have...

1

2

3

4

5

6

7

8

9

10

11

12

13

14

15

16

17

18

19

20

21

22

23

24

25

26

27

28

29

30

31

32

33

Manifest

DATE

/ /

I am so happy and grateful now that I have...

1

2

3

4

5

6

7

8

9

10

11

12

13

14

15

16

17

18

19

20

21

22

23

24

25

26

27

28

29

30

31

32

33

Manifest

DATE

/ /

I am so happy and grateful now that I have...

1 __________
2 __________
3 __________
4 __________
5 __________
6 __________
7 __________
8 __________
9 __________
10 __________
11 __________
12 __________
13 __________
14 __________
15 __________
16 __________
17 __________
18 __________
19 __________
20 __________
21 __________
22 __________
23 __________
24 __________
25 __________
26 __________
27 __________
28 __________
29 __________
30 __________
31 __________
32 __________
33 __________

DATE

/ /

Soul Reflection

3 CHANGES I OBSERVED AFTER MANIFESTING

1 ______________________________

2 ______________________________

3 ______________________________

3 THINGS I LEARNED IN THIS PROCESS?

1 ______________________________

2 ______________________________

3 ______________________________

3 CHALLENGES I FACED?

1 ______________________________

2 ______________________________

3 ______________________________

AFTER MANIFESTING...

I SEE	I FEEL	I HAVE

MANIFESTATION HIGHLIGHTS

Notes

DATE

/ /

extra thoughts

Notes

DATE

/ /

extra thoughts

DATE

/ /

My Vision Board

what I envision my life will look like after this manifestation

career & finances

love & travel

home & family

spiritual & wellness

friends & connections

DATE

/ /

Offer Gratitude

3 THINGS I AM FEELING TODAY

POSITIVE AFFIRMATION

3 THINGS I AM CURRENTLY GRATEFUL FOR

1

2

3

SOMETHING I AM ALREADY PROUD OF

HOW I FEEL NOW	HOW I WANT TO FEEL

MY INTENTION FOR THIS MANIFESTATION

WHY IS THIS MANIFESTATION IMPORTANT TO ME?

Manifest

DATE

/ /

I am so happy and grateful now that I have...

1
2
3
4
5
6
7
8
9
10
11
12
13
14
15
16
17
18
19
20
21
22
23
24
25
26
27
28
29
30
31
32
33

Manifest

DATE

/ /

I am so happy and grateful now that I have...

1
2
3
4
5
6
7
8
9
10
11
12
13
14
15
16
17
18
19
20
21
22
23
24
25
26
27
28
29
30
31
32
33

Manifest

DATE

/ /

I am so happy and grateful now that I have...

1

2

3

4

5

6

7

8

9

10

11

12

13

14

15

16

17

18

19

20

21

22

23

24

25

26

27

28

29

30

31

32

33

DATE

/ /

Soul Reflection

3 CHANGES I OBSERVED AFTER MANIFESTING

1 ____________________

2 ____________________

3 ____________________

3 THINGS I LEARNED IN THIS PROCESS?

1 ____________________

2 ____________________

3 ____________________

3 CHALLENGES I FACED?

1 ____________________

2 ____________________

3 ____________________

AFTER MANIFESTING...

I SEE	I FEEL	I HAVE

MANIFESTATION HIGHLIGHTS

Notes

DATE

/ /

extra thoughts

Notes

DATE

/ /

extra thoughts

DATE

/ /

My Vision Board

what I envision my life will look like after this manifestation

career & finances

love & travel

home & family

spiritual & wellness

friends & connections

DATE

/ /

Offer Gratitude

3 THINGS I AM FEELING TODAY

POSITIVE AFFIRMATION

3 THINGS I AM CURRENTLY GRATEFUL FOR

1

2

3

SOMETHING I AM ALREADY PROUD OF

HOW I FEEL NOW

HOW I WANT TO FEEL

MY INTENTION FOR THIS MANIFESTATION

WHY IS THIS MANIFESTATION IMPORTANT TO ME?

Manifest

DATE

/ /

I am so happy and grateful now that I have...

1
2
3
4
5
6
7
8
9
10
11
12
13
14
15
16
17
18
19
20
21
22
23
24
25
26
27
28
29
30
31
32
33

Manifest

DATE

/ /

I am so happy and grateful now that I have...

1
2
3
4
5
6
7
8
9
10
11
12
13
14
15
16
17
18
19
20
21
22
23
24
25
26
27
28
29
30
31
32
33

Manifest

DATE

/ /

I am so happy and grateful now that I have...

1
2
3
4
5
6
7
8
9
10
11
12
13
14
15
16
17
18
19
20
21
22
23
24
25
26
27
28
29
30
31
32
33

DATE

/ /

Soul Reflection

3 CHANGES I OBSERVED AFTER MANIFESTING

1 ______

2 ______

3 ______

3 THINGS I LEARNED IN THIS PROCESS?

1 ______

2 ______

3 ______

3 CHALLENGES I FACED?

1 ______

2 ______

3 ______

AFTER MANIFESTING...

I SEE	I FEEL	I HAVE

MANIFESTATION HIGHLIGHTS

Notes

DATE

/ /

extra thoughts

Notes

DATE

/ /

extra thoughts

DATE

/ /

My Vision Board

what I envision my life will look like after this manifestation

career & finances

love & travel

home & family

spiritual & wellness

friends & connections

DATE

/ /

Offer Gratitude

3 THINGS I AM FEELING TODAY

POSITIVE AFFIRMATION

3 THINGS I AM CURRENTLY GRATEFUL FOR

1

2

3

SOMETHING I AM ALREADY PROUD OF

HOW I FEEL NOW	HOW I WANT TO FEEL

MY INTENTION FOR THIS MANIFESTATION

WHY IS THIS MANIFESTATION IMPORTANT TO ME?

Manifest

DATE
/ /

I am so happy and grateful now that I have...

1
2
3
4
5
6
7
8
9
10
11
12
13
14
15
16
17
18
19
20
21
22
23
24
25
26
27
28
29
30
31
32
33

Manifest

DATE

/ /

I am so happy and grateful now that I have...

1
2
3
4
5
6
7
8
9
10
11
12
13
14
15
16
17
18
19
20
21
22
23
24
25
26
27
28
29
30
31
32
33

Manifest

DATE

/ /

I am so happy and grateful now that I have...

1
2
3
4
5
6
7
8
9
10
11
12
13
14
15
16
17
18
19
20
21
22
23
24
25
26
27
28
29
30
31
32
33

DATE

/ /

Soul Reflection

3 CHANGES I OBSERVED AFTER MANIFESTING

1 ______________________________

2 ______________________________

3 ______________________________

3 THINGS I LEARNED IN THIS PROCESS?

1 ______________________________

2 ______________________________

3 ______________________________

3 CHALLENGES I FACED?

1 ______________________________

2 ______________________________

3 ______________________________

AFTER MANIFESTING...

I SEE	I FEEL	I HAVE

MANIFESTATION HIGHLIGHTS

Notes

DATE

/ /

extra thoughts

Notes

DATE

/ /

extra thoughts

DATE

/ /

My Vision Board

what I envision my life will look like after this manifestation

career & finances

love & travel

home & family

spiritual & wellness

friends & connections

DATE

/ /

Offer Gratitude

3 THINGS I AM FEELING TODAY

POSITIVE AFFIRMATION

3 THINGS I AM CURRENTLY GRATEFUL FOR

1

2

3

SOMETHING I AM ALREADY PROUD OF

HOW I FEEL NOW

HOW I WANT TO FEEL

MY INTENTION FOR THIS MANIFESTATION

WHY IS THIS MANIFESTATION IMPORTANT TO ME?

Manifest

DATE

/ /

I am so happy and grateful now that I have...

1
2
3
4
5
6
7
8
9
10
11
12
13
14
15
16
17
18
19
20
21
22
23
24
25
26
27
28
29
30
31
32
33

Manifest

DATE

/ /

I am so happy and grateful now that I have...

1

2

3

4

5

6

7

8

9

10

11

12

13

14

15

16

17

18

19

20

21

22

23

24

25

26

27

28

29

30

31

32

33

Manifest

DATE

/ /

I am so happy and grateful now that I have...

1
2
3
4
5
6
7
8
9
10
11
12
13
14
15
16
17
18
19
20
21
22
23
24
25
26
27
28
29
30
31
32
33

DATE

/ /

Soul Reflection

3 CHANGES I OBSERVED AFTER MANIFESTING

1 ______

2 ______

3 ______

3 THINGS I LEARNED IN THIS PROCESS?

1 ______

2 ______

3 ______

3 CHALLENGES I FACED?

1 ______

2 ______

3 ______

AFTER MANIFESTING...

I SEE	I FEEL	I HAVE

MANIFESTATION HIGHLIGHTS

Notes

DATE
/ /

extra thoughts

Notes

DATE

/ /

extra thoughts

DATE

/ /

My Vision Board

what I envision my life will look like after this manifestation

career & finances

love & travel

home & family

spiritual & wellness

friends & connections

DATE
/ /

Offer Gratitude

3 THINGS I AM FEELING TODAY

POSITIVE AFFIRMATION

3 THINGS I AM CURRENTLY GRATEFUL FOR

1

2

3

SOMETHING I AM ALREADY PROUD OF

HOW I FEEL NOW

HOW I WANT TO FEEL

MY INTENTION FOR THIS MANIFESTATION

WHY IS THIS MANIFESTATION IMPORTANT TO ME?

Manifest

DATE

/ /

I am so happy and grateful now that I have...

1 ____
2 ____
3 ____
4 ____
5 ____
6 ____
7 ____
8 ____
9 ____
10 ____
11 ____
12 ____
13 ____
14 ____
15 ____
16 ____
17 ____
18 ____
19 ____
20 ____
21 ____
22 ____
23 ____
24 ____
25 ____
26 ____
27 ____
28 ____
29 ____
30 ____
31 ____
32 ____
33 ____

Manifest

DATE

/ /

I am so happy and grateful now that I have...

1
2
3
4
5
6
7
8
9
10
11
12
13
14
15
16
17
18
19
20
21
22
23
24
25
26
27
28
29
30
31
32
33

Manifest

DATE

/ /

I am so happy and grateful now that I have...

1

2

3

4

5

6

7

8

9

10

11

12

13

14

15

16

17

18

19

20

21

22

23

24

25

26

27

28

29

30

31

32

33

DATE

/ /

Soul Reflection

3 CHANGES I OBSERVED AFTER MANIFESTING

1 ______

2 ______

3 ______

3 THINGS I LEARNED IN THIS PROCESS?

1 ______

2 ______

3 ______

3 CHALLENGES I FACED?

1 ______

2 ______

3 ______

AFTER MANIFESTING...

I SEE	I FEEL	I HAVE

MANIFESTATION HIGHLIGHTS

Notes

DATE

/ /

extra thoughts

Notes

DATE

/ /

extra thoughts

DATE

/ /

My Vision Board

what I envision my life will look like after this manifestation

career & finances

love & travel

home & family

spiritual & wellness

friends & connections

DATE

/ /

Offer Gratitude

3 THINGS I AM FEELING TODAY

POSITIVE AFFIRMATION

3 THINGS I AM CURRENTLY GRATEFUL FOR

1

2

3

SOMETHING I AM ALREADY PROUD OF

HOW I FEEL NOW

HOW I WANT TO FEEL

MY INTENTION FOR THIS MANIFESTATION

WHY IS THIS MANIFESTATION IMPORTANT TO ME?

Manifest

DATE

/ /

I am so happy and grateful now that I have...

1
2
3
4
5
6
7
8
9
10
11
12
13
14
15
16
17
18
19
20
21
22
23
24
25
26
27
28
29
30
31
32
33

Manifest

DATE

/ /

I am so happy and grateful now that I have...

1

2

3

4

5

6

7

8

9

10

11

12

13

14

15

16

17

18

19

20

21

22

23

24

25

26

27

28

29

30

31

32

33

Manifest

DATE

/ /

I am so happy and grateful now that I have...

1
2
3
4
5
6
7
8
9
10
11
12
13
14
15
16
17
18
19
20
21
22
23
24
25
26
27
28
29
30
31
32
33

DATE

/ /

Soul Reflection

3 CHANGES I OBSERVED AFTER MANIFESTING

1 ____________________

2 ____________________

3 ____________________

3 THINGS I LEARNED IN THIS PROCESS?

1 ____________________

2 ____________________

3 ____________________

3 CHALLENGES I FACED?

1 ____________________

2 ____________________

3 ____________________

AFTER MANIFESTING...

I SEE	I FEEL	I HAVE

MANIFESTATION HIGHLIGHTS

Notes

DATE

/ /

extra thoughts

Notes

DATE

/ /

extra thoughts

DATE

/ /

My Vision Board

what I envision my life will look like after this manifestation

career & finances

love & travel

home & family

spiritual & wellness

friends & connections

DATE

/ /

Offer Gratitude

3 THINGS I AM FEELING TODAY

POSITIVE AFFIRMATION

3 THINGS I AM CURRENTLY GRATEFUL FOR

1 ______

2 ______

3 ______

SOMETHING I AM ALREADY PROUD OF

______

HOW I FEEL NOW	HOW I WANT TO FEEL

MY INTENTION FOR THIS MANIFESTATION

______

______

WHY IS THIS MANIFESTATION IMPORTANT TO ME?

Manifest

DATE

/ /

I am so happy and grateful now that I have...

1
2
3
4
5
6
7
8
9
10
11
12
13
14
15
16
17
18
19
20
21
22
23
24
25
26
27
28
29
30
31
32
33

Manifest

DATE

/ /

I am so happy and grateful now that I have...

1
2
3
4
5
6
7
8
9
10
11
12
13
14
15
16
17
18
19
20
21
22
23
24
25
26
27
28
29
30
31
32
33

Manifest

DATE

/ /

I am so happy and grateful now that I have...

1
2
3
4
5
6
7
8
9
10
11
12
13
14
15
16
17
18
19
20
21
22
23
24
25
26
27
28
29
30
31
32
33

DATE

/ /

Soul Reflection

3 CHANGES I OBSERVED AFTER MANIFESTING

1 ______________________________

2 ______________________________

3 ______________________________

3 THINGS I LEARNED IN THIS PROCESS?

1 ______________________________

2 ______________________________

3 ______________________________

3 CHALLENGES I FACED?

1 ______________________________

2 ______________________________

3 ______________________________

AFTER MANIFESTING...

I SEE	I FEEL	I HAVE

MANIFESTATION HIGHLIGHTS

Notes

DATE

/ /

extra thoughts

Notes

DATE

/ /

extra thoughts

DATE

/ /

My Vision Board

what I envision my life will look like after this manifestation

career & finances

love & travel

home & family

spiritual & wellness

friends & connections

DATE

/ /

Offer Gratitude

3 THINGS I AM FEELING TODAY

POSITIVE AFFIRMATION

3 THINGS I AM CURRENTLY GRATEFUL FOR

1 ____________________

2 ____________________

3 ____________________

SOMETHING I AM ALREADY PROUD OF

HOW I FEEL NOW

HOW I WANT TO FEEL

MY INTENTION FOR THIS MANIFESTATION

WHY IS THIS MANIFESTATION IMPORTANT TO ME?

Manifest

DATE

/ /

I am so happy and grateful now that I have...

1
2
3
4
5
6
7
8
9
10
11
12
13
14
15
16
17
18
19
20
21
22
23
24
25
26
27
28
29
30
31
32
33

Manifest

DATE

/ /

I am so happy and grateful now that I have...

1

2

3

4

5

6

7

8

9

10

11

12

13

14

15

16

17

18

19

20

21

22

23

24

25

26

27

28

29

30

31

32

33

Manifest

DATE

/ /

I am so happy and grateful now that I have...

1

2

3

4

5

6

7

8

9

10

11

12

13

14

15

16

17

18

19

20

21

22

23

24

25

26

27

28

29

30

31

32

33

DATE

/ /

Soul Reflection

3 CHANGES I OBSERVED AFTER MANIFESTING

1 ______

2 ______

3 ______

3 THINGS I LEARNED IN THIS PROCESS?

1 ______

2 ______

3 ______

3 CHALLENGES I FACED?

1 ______

2 ______

3 ______

AFTER MANIFESTING...

I SEE	I FEEL	I HAVE

MANIFESTATION HIGHLIGHTS

Notes

DATE

/ /

extra thoughts

Notes

DATE

/ /

extra thoughts

DATE

/ /

My Vision Board

what I envision my life will look like after this manifestation

career & finances

love & travel

home & family

spiritual & wellness

friends & connections

DATE

/ /

Offer Gratitude

3 THINGS I AM FEELING TODAY

POSITIVE AFFIRMATION

3 THINGS I AM CURRENTLY GRATEFUL FOR

1 __________

2 __________

3 __________

SOMETHING I AM ALREADY PROUD OF

HOW I FEEL NOW

HOW I WANT TO FEEL

MY INTENTION FOR THIS MANIFESTATION

WHY IS THIS MANIFESTATION IMPORTANT TO ME?

Manifest

DATE

/ /

I am so happy and grateful now that I have...

1

2

3

4

5

6

7

8

9

10

11

12

13

14

15

16

17

18

19

20

21

22

23

24

25

26

27

28

29

30

31

32

33

Manifest

DATE

/ /

I am so happy and grateful now that I have...

1
2
3
4
5
6
7
8
9
10
11
12
13
14
15
16
17
18
19
20
21
22
23
24
25
26
27
28
29
30
31
32
33

Manifest

DATE

/ /

I am so happy and grateful now that I have...

1
2
3
4
5
6
7
8
9
10
11
12
13
14
15
16
17
18
19
20
21
22
23
24
25
26
27
28
29
30
31
32
33

DATE

/ /

Soul Reflection

3 CHANGES I OBSERVED AFTER MANIFESTING

1 ______

2 ______

3 ______

3 THINGS I LEARNED IN THIS PROCESS?

1 ______

2 ______

3 ______

3 CHALLENGES I FACED?

1 ______

2 ______

3 ______

AFTER MANIFESTING...

I SEE	I FEEL	I HAVE

MANIFESTATION HIGHLIGHTS

Notes

DATE

/ /

extra thoughts

Notes

DATE

/ /

extra thoughts

DATE

/ /

My Vision Board

what I envision my life will look like after this manifestation

career & finances

love & travel

home & family

spiritual & wellness

friends & connections

DATE

/ /

Offer Gratitude

3 THINGS I AM FEELING TODAY

POSITIVE AFFIRMATION

3 THINGS I AM CURRENTLY GRATEFUL FOR

1

2

3

SOMETHING I AM ALREADY PROUD OF

HOW I FEEL NOW

HOW I WANT TO FEEL

MY INTENTION FOR THIS MANIFESTATION

WHY IS THIS MANIFESTATION IMPORTANT TO ME?

Manifest

DATE

/ /

I am so happy and grateful now that I have...

1

2

3

4

5

6

7

8

9

10

11

12

13

14

15

16

17

18

19

20

21

22

23

24

25

26

27

28

29

30

31

32

33

Manifest

DATE

/ /

I am so happy and grateful now that I have...

1 ______

2 ______

3 ______

4 ______

5 ______

6 ______

7 ______

8 ______

9 ______

10 ______

11 ______

12 ______

13 ______

14 ______

15 ______

16 ______

17 ______

18 ______

19 ______

20 ______

21 ______

22 ______

23 ______

24 ______

25 ______

26 ______

27 ______

28 ______

29 ______

30 ______

31 ______

32 ______

33 ______

Manifest

DATE

/ /

I am so happy and grateful now that I have...

1

2

3

4

5

6

7

8

9

10

11

12

13

14

15

16

17

18

19

20

21

22

23

24

25

26

27

28

29

30

31

32

33

DATE

/ /

Soul Reflection

3 CHANGES I OBSERVED AFTER MANIFESTING

1 __________

2 __________

3 __________

3 THINGS I LEARNED IN THIS PROCESS?

1 __________

2 __________

3 __________

3 CHALLENGES I FACED?

1 __________

2 __________

3 __________

AFTER MANIFESTING...

I SEE	I FEEL	I HAVE

MANIFESTATION HIGHLIGHTS

Notes

DATE

/ /

extra thoughts

Notes

DATE

/ /

extra thoughts

DATE

/ /

My Vision Board

what I envision my life will look like after this manifestation

career & finances

love & travel

home & family

spiritual & wellness

friends & connections

DATE

/ /

Offer Gratitude

3 THINGS I AM FEELING TODAY

POSITIVE AFFIRMATION

3 THINGS I AM CURRENTLY GRATEFUL FOR

1 ______

2 ______

3 ______

SOMETHING I AM ALREADY PROUD OF

______

HOW I FEEL NOW

HOW I WANT TO FEEL

MY INTENTION FOR THIS MANIFESTATION

______

______

WHY IS THIS MANIFESTATION IMPORTANT TO ME?

Manifest

DATE

/ /

I am so happy and grateful now that I have...

1

2

3

4

5

6

7

8

9

10

11

12

13

14

15

16

17

18

19

20

21

22

23

24

25

26

27

28

29

30

31

32

33

Manifest

DATE

/ /

I am so happy and grateful now that I have...

1
2
3
4
5
6
7
8
9
10
11
12
13
14
15
16
17
18
19
20
21
22
23
24
25
26
27
28
29
30
31
32
33

Manifest

DATE

/ /

I am so happy and grateful now that I have...

1

2

3

4

5

6

7

8

9

10

11

12

13

14

15

16

17

18

19

20

21

22

23

24

25

26

27

28

29

30

31

32

33

DATE

/ /

Soul Reflection

3 CHANGES I OBSERVED AFTER MANIFESTING

1 ______________________________

2 ______________________________

3 ______________________________

3 THINGS I LEARNED IN THIS PROCESS?

1 ______________________________

2 ______________________________

3 ______________________________

3 CHALLENGES I FACED?

1 ______________________________

2 ______________________________

3 ______________________________

AFTER MANIFESTING...

I SEE	I FEEL	I HAVE

MANIFESTATION HIGHLIGHTS

Notes

DATE

/ /

extra thoughts

Notes

DATE

/ /

extra thoughts

DATE

/ /

My Vision Board

what I envision my life will look like after this manifestation

career & finances

love & travel

home & family

spiritual & wellness

friends & connections

DATE

/ /

Offer Gratitude

3 THINGS I AM FEELING TODAY

POSITIVE AFFIRMATION

3 THINGS I AM CURRENTLY GRATEFUL FOR

1 ____________________

2 ____________________

3 ____________________

SOMETHING I AM ALREADY PROUD OF

HOW I FEEL NOW

HOW I WANT TO FEEL

MY INTENTION FOR THIS MANIFESTATION

WHY IS THIS MANIFESTATION IMPORTANT TO ME?

Manifest

DATE

/ /

I am so happy and grateful now that I have...

Manifest

DATE

/ /

I am so happy and grateful now that I have...

1
2
3
4
5
6
7
8
9
10
11
12
13
14
15
16
17
18
19
20
21
22
23
24
25
26
27
28
29
30
31
32
33

Manifest

DATE

/ /

I am so happy and grateful now that I have...

1
2
3
4
5
6
7
8
9
10
11
12
13
14
15
16
17
18
19
20
21
22
23
24
25
26
27
28
29
30
31
32
33

DATE

/ /

Soul Reflection

3 CHANGES I OBSERVED AFTER MANIFESTING

1 ______________________________

2 ______________________________

3 ______________________________

3 THINGS I LEARNED IN THIS PROCESS?

1 ______________________________

2 ______________________________

3 ______________________________

3 CHALLENGES I FACED?

1 ______________________________

2 ______________________________

3 ______________________________

AFTER MANIFESTING...

I SEE	I FEEL	I HAVE

MANIFESTATION HIGHLIGHTS

Notes

DATE
/ /

extra thoughts

Notes

DATE

/ /

extra thoughts

DATE

/ /

My Vision Board

what I envision my life will look like after this manifestation

career & finances

love & travel

home & family

spiritual & wellness

friends & connections

DATE

/ /

Offer Gratitude

3 THINGS I AM FEELING TODAY

POSITIVE AFFIRMATION

3 THINGS I AM CURRENTLY GRATEFUL FOR

1

2

3

SOMETHING I AM ALREADY PROUD OF

HOW I FEEL NOW

HOW I WANT TO FEEL

MY INTENTION FOR THIS MANIFESTATION

WHY IS THIS MANIFESTATION IMPORTANT TO ME?

Manifest

DATE

/ /

I am so happy and grateful now that I have...

1
2
3
4
5
6
7
8
9
10
11
12
13
14
15
16
17
18
19
20
21
22
23
24
25
26
27
28
29
30
31
32
33

Manifest

DATE

/ /

I am so happy and grateful now that I have...

1
2
3
4
5
6
7
8
9
10
11
12
13
14
15
16
17
18
19
20
21
22
23
24
25
26
27
28
29
30
31
32
33

Manifest

DATE

/ /

I am so happy and grateful now that I have...

1
2
3
4
5
6
7
8
9
10
11
12
13
14
15
16
17
18
19
20
21
22
23
24
25
26
27
28
29
30
31
32
33

DATE

/ /

Soul Reflection

3 CHANGES I OBSERVED AFTER MANIFESTING

1 ______

2 ______

3 ______

3 THINGS I LEARNED IN THIS PROCESS?

1 ______

2 ______

3 ______

3 CHALLENGES I FACED?

1 ______

2 ______

3 ______

AFTER MANIFESTING...

I SEE	I FEEL	I HAVE

MANIFESTATION HIGHLIGHTS

Notes

DATE

/ /

extra thoughts

Notes

DATE
/ /

extra thoughts

DATE

/ /

My Vision Board

what I envision my life will look like after this manifestation

career & finances

love & travel

home & family

spiritual & wellness

friends & connections

DATE

/ /

Offer Gratitude

3 THINGS I AM FEELING TODAY

POSITIVE AFFIRMATION

3 THINGS I AM CURRENTLY GRATEFUL FOR

1

2

3

SOMETHING I AM ALREADY PROUD OF

HOW I FEEL NOW

HOW I WANT TO FEEL

MY INTENTION FOR THIS MANIFESTATION

WHY IS THIS MANIFESTATION IMPORTANT TO ME?

Manifest

DATE
/ /

I am so happy and grateful now that I have...

1
2
3
4
5
6
7
8
9
10
11
12
13
14
15
16
17
18
19
20
21
22
23
24
25
26
27
28
29
30
31
32
33

Manifest

DATE

/ /

I am so happy and grateful now that I have...

1

2

3

4

5

6

7

8

9

10

11

12

13

14

15

16

17

18

19

20

21

22

23

24

25

26

27

28

29

30

31

32

33

Manifest

DATE

/ /

I am so happy and grateful now that I have...

1 __________

2 __________

3 __________

4 __________

5 __________

6 __________

7 __________

8 __________

9 __________

10 __________

11 __________

12 __________

13 __________

14 __________

15 __________

16 __________

17 __________

18 __________

19 __________

20 __________

21 __________

22 __________

23 __________

24 __________

25 __________

26 __________

27 __________

28 __________

29 __________

30 __________

31 __________

32 __________

33 __________

DATE

/ /

Soul Reflection

3 CHANGES I OBSERVED AFTER MANIFESTING

1 __________

2 __________

3 __________

3 THINGS I LEARNED IN THIS PROCESS?

1 __________

2 __________

3 __________

3 CHALLENGES I FACED?

1 __________

2 __________

3 __________

AFTER MANIFESTING...

I SEE	I FEEL	I HAVE

MANIFESTATION HIGHLIGHTS

Notes

DATE

/ /

extra thoughts

Notes

DATE

/ /

extra thoughts

DATE

/ /

My Vision Board

what I envision my life will look like after this manifestation

career & finances

love & travel

home & family

spiritual & wellness

friends & connections

DATE

/ /

Offer Gratitude

3 THINGS I AM FEELING TODAY

POSITIVE AFFIRMATION

3 THINGS I AM CURRENTLY GRATEFUL FOR

1

2

3

SOMETHING I AM ALREADY PROUD OF

HOW I FEEL NOW	HOW I WANT TO FEEL

MY INTENTION FOR THIS MANIFESTATION

WHY IS THIS MANIFESTATION IMPORTANT TO ME?

Manifest

DATE

/ /

I am so happy and grateful now that I have...

1
2
3
4
5
6
7
8
9
10
11
12
13
14
15
16
17
18
19
20
21
22
23
24
25
26
27
28
29
30
31
32
33

Manifest

DATE

/ /

I am so happy and grateful now that I have...

1
2
3
4
5
6
7
8
9
10
11
12
13
14
15
16
17
18
19
20
21
22
23
24
25
26
27
28
29
30
31
32
33

Manifest

DATE

/ /

I am so happy and grateful now that I have...

1
2
3
4
5
6
7
8
9
10
11
12
13
14
15
16
17
18
19
20
21
22
23
24
25
26
27
28
29
30
31
32
33

DATE

/ /

Soul Reflection

3 CHANGES I OBSERVED AFTER MANIFESTING

1 ____________________

2 ____________________

3 ____________________

3 THINGS I LEARNED IN THIS PROCESS?

1 ____________________

2 ____________________

3 ____________________

3 CHALLENGES I FACED?

1 ____________________

2 ____________________

3 ____________________

AFTER MANIFESTING...

I SEE	I FEEL	I HAVE

MANIFESTATION HIGHLIGHTS

Notes

DATE

/ /

extra thoughts

Notes

DATE

/ /

extra thoughts

DATE

/ /

My Vision Board

what I envision my life will look like after this manifestation

career & finances

love & travel

home & family

spiritual & wellness

friends & connections

DATE

/ /

Offer Gratitude

3 THINGS I AM FEELING TODAY

POSITIVE AFFIRMATION

3 THINGS I AM CURRENTLY GRATEFUL FOR

1 ______

2 ______

3 ______

SOMETHING I AM ALREADY PROUD OF

______

HOW I FEEL NOW	HOW I WANT TO FEEL

MY INTENTION FOR THIS MANIFESTATION

______

______

WHY IS THIS MANIFESTATION IMPORTANT TO ME?

Manifest

DATE

/ /

I am so happy and grateful now that I have...

1

2

3

4

5

6

7

8

9

10

11

12

13

14

15

16

17

18

19

20

21

22

23

24

25

26

27

28

29

30

31

32

33

Manifest

DATE

/ /

I am so happy and grateful now that I have...

1
2
3
4
5
6
7
8
9
10
11
12
13
14
15
16
17
18
19
20
21
22
23
24
25
26
27
28
29
30
31
32
33

Manifest

DATE

/ /

I am so happy and grateful now that I have...

1

2

3

4

5

6

7

8

9

10

11

12

13

14

15

16

17

18

19

20

21

22

23

24

25

26

27

28

29

30

31

32

33

DATE

/ /

Soul Reflection

3 CHANGES I OBSERVED AFTER MANIFESTING

1 ______

2 ______

3 ______

3 THINGS I LEARNED IN THIS PROCESS?

1 ______

2 ______

3 ______

3 CHALLENGES I FACED?

1 ______

2 ______

3 ______

AFTER MANIFESTING...

I SEE	I FEEL	I HAVE

MANIFESTATION HIGHLIGHTS

Notes

DATE

/ /

extra thoughts

Notes

DATE

/ /

extra thoughts

DATE

/ /

My Vision Board

what I envision my life will look like after this manifestation

career & finances

love & travel

home & family

spiritual & wellness

friends & connections

DATE

/ /

Offer Gratitude

3 THINGS I AM FEELING TODAY

POSITIVE AFFIRMATION

3 THINGS I AM CURRENTLY GRATEFUL FOR

1

2

3

SOMETHING I AM ALREADY PROUD OF

HOW I FEEL NOW

HOW I WANT TO FEEL

MY INTENTION FOR THIS MANIFESTATION

WHY IS THIS MANIFESTATION IMPORTANT TO ME?

Manifest

DATE

/ /

I am so happy and grateful now that I have...

1 __________
2 __________
3 __________
4 __________
5 __________
6 __________
7 __________
8 __________
9 __________
10 __________
11 __________
12 __________
13 __________
14 __________
15 __________
16 __________
17 __________
18 __________
19 __________
20 __________
21 __________
22 __________
23 __________
24 __________
25 __________
26 __________
27 __________
28 __________
29 __________
30 __________
31 __________
32 __________
33 __________

Manifest

DATE

/ /

I am so happy and grateful now that I have...

1 __________
2 __________
3 __________
4 __________
5 __________
6 __________
7 __________
8 __________
9 __________
10 __________
11 __________
12 __________
13 __________
14 __________
15 __________
16 __________
17 __________
18 __________
19 __________
20 __________
21 __________
22 __________
23 __________
24 __________
25 __________
26 __________
27 __________
28 __________
29 __________
30 __________
31 __________
32 __________
33 __________

Manifest

DATE
/ /

I am so happy and grateful now that I have...

1
2
3
4
5
6
7
8
9
10
11
12
13
14
15
16
17
18
19
20
21
22
23
24
25
26
27
28
29
30
31
32
33

DATE

/ /

Soul Reflection

3 CHANGES I OBSERVED AFTER MANIFESTING

1 ______________________________

2 ______________________________

3 ______________________________

3 THINGS I LEARNED IN THIS PROCESS?

1 ______________________________

2 ______________________________

3 ______________________________

3 CHALLENGES I FACED?

1 ______________________________

2 ______________________________

3 ______________________________

AFTER MANIFESTING...

I SEE	I FEEL	I HAVE

MANIFESTATION HIGHLIGHTS

Notes

DATE

/ /

extra thoughts

Notes

DATE
/ /

extra thoughts

DATE

/ /

My Vision Board

what I envision my life will look like after this manifestation

career & finances

love & travel

home & family

spiritual & wellness

friends & connections

DATE

/ /

Offer Gratitude

3 THINGS I AM FEELING TODAY

POSITIVE AFFIRMATION

3 THINGS I AM CURRENTLY GRATEFUL FOR

1 ______

2 ______

3 ______

SOMETHING I AM ALREADY PROUD OF

______

HOW I FEEL NOW	HOW I WANT TO FEEL

MY INTENTION FOR THIS MANIFESTATION

______

______

WHY IS THIS MANIFESTATION IMPORTANT TO ME?

Manifest

DATE

/ /

I am so happy and grateful now that I have...

1

2

3

4

5

6

7

8

9

10

11

12

13

14

15

16

17

18

19

20

21

22

23

24

25

26

27

28

29

30

31

32

33

Manifest

DATE

/ /

I am so happy and grateful now that I have...

1
2
3
4
5
6
7
8
9
10
11
12
13
14
15
16
17
18
19
20
21
22
23
24
25
26
27
28
29
30
31
32
33

Manifest

DATE

/ /

I am so happy and grateful now that I have...

1
2
3
4
5
6
7
8
9
10
11
12
13
14
15
16
17
18
19
20
21
22
23
24
25
26
27
28
29
30
31
32
33

DATE

/ /

Soul Reflection

3 CHANGES I OBSERVED AFTER MANIFESTING

1 ______

2 ______

3 ______

3 THINGS I LEARNED IN THIS PROCESS?

1 ______

2 ______

3 ______

3 CHALLENGES I FACED?

1 ______

2 ______

3 ______

AFTER MANIFESTING...

I SEE	I FEEL	I HAVE

MANIFESTATION HIGHLIGHTS

Notes

DATE

/ /

extra thoughts